I find television very educational.
Every time someone switches it on,
I go into another room and read a good book.
—Groucho Marx

BUDDHIST BOOT CAMP

by Timber Hawkeye

HarperOne
An Imprint of HarperCollinsPublishers

HarperOne

HarperCollins books may be purchased for educational, business, or sales
promotional use. For information, please e-mail the Special Markets Department
at SPsales@harpercollins.com.

"Buddhist Boot Camp" and "Sit Happens"
are both Registered Trademarks held by Sit Happens, LLC.

HarperCollins website: http://www.harpercollins.com

HarperCollins®, ♦®, and HarperOne™ are
trademarks of HarperCollins Publishers.

Photographs by Rodel Casio.

FIRST HARPERCOLLINS EDITION

Previously self-published.

Library of Congress Cataloging-in-Publication Data is available upon request.

ISBN 978–0–06–226743–6

13 14 15 16 17 RRD(H) 10

Basic Training

The chapters in this book are short and easy to understand,
and can be read in any order.

LIVING IN GRATITUDE

The intention is to awaken, enlighten,
enrich and inspire.

BUDDHIST BOOT CAMP

This book is dedicated to you.

To make a long story short . . .

I sat there in front of the Tibetan Lama, wearing my maroon robes after years of studying Buddhism. "With all due respect," I said, "I don't believe the Buddha ever intended for his teachings to get THIS complicated!"

My teacher looked around at all the statues of deities with multiple arms and chuckled, "The Buddha didn't do this! The Tibetan culture did; this is their way. Why don't you try Zen? I think you'd like it!"

So I bowed out of the temple, took off my robes, and moved into a Zen monastery far from home. Zen was simpler; that much was true (the walls were blank and I loved it), but the teachings were still filled with all the dogma that sent me running from religion in the first place.

There are many incredible books out there that cover all aspects of religion, philosophy, psychology and physics, but I was looking for something less "academic," so to speak. I was looking for something inspirational that people today would not only have the attention span to read all the way through, but actually understand and also implement in their daily lives. I pictured a simple guide to being happy, and in it just two words: "Be Grateful."

Gratitude has a way of turning what we have into enough, and that is the basic idea behind *Buddhist Boot Camp*.

The short chapters convey everything I have learned over the years in a way that is easy to understand, without you needing to know anything about Buddhism ahead of time. In fact, this book is not about being a Buddhist; it's about being a Buddha.

It is very possible (and perfectly okay) for someone who is Catholic, Muslim, Atheist or Jewish, for example, to still find the Buddha's teachings inspirational. You can love Jesus, repeat a Hindu mantra, and still go to temple after morning meditation. Buddhism is not a threat to any religion, it actually strengthens your existing faith by expanding your love to include all beings.

"Boot Camp" is a training method, and Buddhism is all about training the mind. Many people claim they don't have time to meditate every morning, but still want spiritual guidance without any dogma or rituals attached. That is exactly what *Buddhist Boot Camp* provides in this quick and easy-to-digest format.

You are now a soldier of peace in the army of love; welcome to *Buddhist Boot Camp*!

Your brother,
Timber Hawkeye

MINDFULNESS

Grasping

Just as we habitually hoard old birthday cards and souvenirs, bank statements and receipts, clothes, broken appliances and old magazines, we also hang on to pride, anger, outdated opinions and fears.

If we're so attached to tangible things, imagine how difficult letting go of opinions must be (let alone opening our minds to new ideas, perspectives, possibilities and futures). Our beliefs inevitably solidify to be the only truth and reality that we know, which puts a greater distance between us and anyone whose beliefs are different. This distance not only segregates us, it feeds our pride.

All of this grasping, by the way, stems from fear.

Why are we so terrified of change, strangers, the new or the unknown? Has the world not continually shown us beauty, sincerity and love through every generation? Are we so focused on the darkness that we no longer see or even remember the light? This is like *The NeverEnding Story*, if you remember it, wherein the minute people stop believing in a reality, it ceases to exist.

Love is real, people! And it's all around us. It vibrates beneath every act of kindness, service, art and family.

Fear is also very real; it permeates every doubt, despair, hesitation, hatred, jealousy, anger, pride and deceit.

Habitually contemplate whether your thoughts stem from love or from fear. If your thoughts originate in love, then follow them. But if they originate from a place of fear, then dig deep to find the root of your fear. Only then will you be able to finally let go of it so that fear no longer limits your possibilities.

There's nothing to complain about, no reason to be afraid, and everything is possible if we live FOR each other.

As far as I'm concerned, anything not meant to benefit others is simply not worth undertaking.

All the happiness in the world
stems from wanting others to be happy,
and all the suffering in the world
stems from wanting the self to be happy.
—Shantideva

Training the Mind

Your mind is like a spoiled rich kid! You have raised it to think whatever it wants, whenever it wants to and for however long, with no regard for consequence or gratitude. And now that your mind is all grown, it never listens to you! In fact, sometimes you want to focus on something, but your mind keeps drifting away to whatever IT wants to think about. Other times, when you really want to stop thinking about something, your mind "can't help it."

Training the mind means being in charge of your decisions instead of succumbing to cravings and so-called "uncontrollable urges." Can you think of a better method for training a spoiled rich kid than some serious boot camp?

First things first: stop granting yourself everything you crave. Doing so simply conditions the spoiled kid to know that it can continue having whatever it wants.

Please do not mistake this for deprivation, because that's not what I'm suggesting. You can still have ice cream, for example, but only when you decide to, not when a craving "takes over." There is a difference.

So when a thought arises, just watch it; don't react to it. "Oh, I really want ice cream" . . . that's nice; see what it's like to want something but not always get it.

The first few times that you try to train your mind you will see the little kid in you throw a tantrum, which is actually hilarious. But it's understandable; you've never said "no" to it before. It's time you start!

You will eventually notice that you actually have more freedom to choose once you're in control of your choices. It's tricky; I just hope this chapter makes sense.

Things turn out best

for those who make the best

of the way things turn out.

—Art Linkletter

The Big Picture

We are urgently rushing toward some goal or dream, or an ever-elusive "finish line" of some sort. Under the pretense of pursuing happiness (and the heavy weight of questions like "Where do you see yourself five years from now?"), we imagine a different version of ourselves existing in the distant future somewhere—often richer, calmer, stable and wise.

As a result, we spend very little time appreciating where we are today. By being so focused on how things "could be," we are under-appreciating how great things already are.

Unfortunately, this mindset affects how we approach almost everything else in life: instead of being grateful for what we already have, we exhaust ourselves with cravings and longings for what we haven't yet achieved; and rather than seeing the beauty and blessing of the friendships and relationships in our lives (and how fortunate we are to have them in the first place), we regard them as inferior to the imaginary versions we've created of them in our minds.

If we give ourselves very little credit for how far we've already come, we tend to give others little to no credit for their own efforts in life. When we're impatient with ourselves, how can we possibly be forgiving of others? And as long as we continue judging ourselves when we look in the mirror, we'll be doing the same to everyone around us.

Wouldn't it be great to stop, if only for a minute on a regular basis, and reflect on how wonderful everything is?

Pause for a moment and honor the progress you've already made in your life, acknowledge the gifts you DO have, and appreciate life itself for a few breaths.

We are continually evolving, growing, learning and expanding. And let's face it, we will never be "done."

Take a step back and notice how the small details we fret about seem to disappear when we look at the big picture.

I may not have gone where I intended to go,
but I think I have ended up where I needed to be.
—Douglas Adams

Life Is a Piece of Cake

When a friend recently asked me if there is anything I would change about my life, I instinctively said, "Absolutely not! I am more content than I've ever been, and happier than I ever thought would be possible."

His response was, "Surely you would like to have more money, a bigger house or SOMETHING, no?" And my answer to that was . . . "No." I mean, I am already happy; who knows what more money would do to my life?!

It's like this: if life is a cake recipe that we are trying to perfect, then I've got my recipe down JUST RIGHT for the time being (with the ideal amount of flour, sugar, baking soda, etc.). More sugar, for example, would not necessarily make a better cake. In fact, it might ruin it!

So if you're not happy with your life, figure out which ingredients make it bitter and take them out. Don't believe commercials that tell you to spread more frosting on the top, because then you would simply wind up with a bitter cake that has frosting on it.

People say things like, "If I just go on vacation to Hawaii, then my life will be better!" The problem is that when you return home from the Islands (or, in other words, when you're done licking the frosting), your bitter cake will still be there waiting for you.

But, and this is the really good part, if you get the ingredients JUST RIGHT, then your life is awesome (with or without frosting). Anything fun you do on top of that is, well, icing on the cake!

We get to try a new recipe every morning (especially if we live our lives to the fullest). So even if your cake ends up bitter one day, that's okay—make it differently tomorrow. Just never blame other people if your cake doesn't turn out; we each bake our own.

Here's a secret: while everyone's recipe is a little different, the main ingredients for a successful batter are love, gratitude, kindness and patience. And the single most common ingredient that makes people's cake bitter is fear, so don't use it!

Happy baking, everybody!

> If we always do what we've always done, we will always be who we've always been.
>
> —Anonymous

Less Is More

My dad wanted to see what my life was like after years of hearing me talk about simplifying and being a minimalist. I told him that to TRULY understand it, he'd have to come live with me for a month, so he did.

He is very much the materialistic consumer, so when he first walked into my little apartment he said, "OMG! You don't have anything!"

After living with me for a month, however, preparing my meals with me, going for long walks every day, reading, writing, meeting with people one-on-one, and truly tasting the simplicity of my life, he hugged me before boarding his flight back home and said, "There is nothing missing from your life!"

It brought tears to my eyes because he actually got it. Both his statements were true: I don't have anything (in the materialistic sense), yet there is nothing missing from my life.

When I shared this particular story on *Buddhist Boot Camp*'s Facebook page, I received hundreds of wonderful comments from readers who truly understood the significance of that moment with my dad.

Working part-time so that I can live full-time is the best decision I've ever made. I don't feel like I have "sacrificed" a life of "luxury"; I've simply exchanged material goods and the illusion of abundance for actual, true bliss.

I moved apartments every six months when I was younger, so I learned not to keep ANYTHING that I would later have to pack. No knickknacks, no souvenirs, no "stuff."

It feels great to be so light and free from any attachment to things. But if you're torn about throwing or giving away something that has a memory attached to it, keep in mind that you're only giving away the object, not the memory.

If you're worried about not remembering something, take a picture of it (the photo doesn't take up any room). The past will let go of you if you let go of the past.

Now spread your wings and fly!

You don't have anything,
yet there is nothing missing from your life.

—My dad

Unlearn

I'm not sure if wisdom is so much about acquiring additional knowledge, or more about letting go of the illusion that we know any ultimate truths.

My dad made an interesting observation when I explained my life journey to him. "You're not trying to learn anything new," he said. "You're trying to go back to being two years old, aren't you?"

To some degree, I think that's true. I mean, I didn't know how to be prejudiced or judgmental at that age. I was fascinated by everybody regardless of race, weight, height, gender or even species.

In fact, I think everybody is born caring and compassionate, with the capacity to unconditionally love all sentient beings without exception. As soon as we are old enough, however, our parents, teachers, preachers, and society teach us to only love and trust family members or, at most, people with the same colored skin.

As a result, by the time we reach high school, we're so disconnected from one another that we can watch an entire nation starving on TV and not feel an ounce of compassion simply because they don't look like us. It's sometimes not until after college (if at all) that we wake up to realize, "Hey, wait a minute. They're people too!"

I admit having felt very distant from people who were "different" from me in my preteen years. But we certainly don't have to stay who we were when we were younger! I can't even watch a caught fish flopping on the sand without feeling its agony nowadays, let alone see another human in pain.

Sometimes life isn't about anything new that we have to learn, but about what we have to UNlearn instead.

I am another you, and you are another me. And the journey continues. Namaste.

It is easier to build strong children
than to repair broken men.
—Frederick Douglass

Sit Happens

Life can be like a loud football stadium, with all the visual and auditory stimuli of a game (the screaming, laughter, cheering, food, noisemakers, players, refs, and the vibration of your seat . . .).

Now imagine the same stadium absolutely silent, still and calm, to a point where you can hear a person whispering at the other end of the field. That's how I can best explain the transformation of my world through sitting meditation. By lowering the volume, I went from hearing the music of life, to listening to the sounds that make up the song; from living, to being alive.

The true beauty is that it's ongoing . . . it keeps getting better. My senses are heightened and I notice even the subtlest internal changes. There are no words to describe how profound and incredible this feels; one must experience it to truly understand, if only for a moment.

Sitting very still may not sound interesting, but the results of doing it on a daily basis are extraordinary. Is peace merely the absence of war, or is it tranquility despite the conflict? Is happiness the absence of suffering, or is it contentment despite the imperfections?

I believe we can be happy in a world that is already broken, and have inner peace in the midst of chaos. We can be in a frustrating situation but choose not to get frustrated, and we can also find bliss in less-than-ideal situations. Happiness is a choice.

When the mind's delight in being stimulated is exhausted, serenity sets in . . . a deep calm with a half-smile of appreciation and acceptance of whatever arises, without judgment or aversion. It's a sense of relief beyond peacefulness; it is divine tranquility.

Through meditation
and by giving full attention to
one thing at a time,
we can learn to direct attention
where we choose.
—Eknath Easwaran

We Are the Victims of Our Own Choices

Where we are today is a direct result of decisions we've made as far back as ten years or lifetimes ago, and as recently as last night.

We have a tremendous personal responsibility for the way our life has turned out, and an equally important role of steering it into the future. Although we constantly make decisions, we're not always mindful of their far-reaching consequences.

The first step is to have a very clear idea of the kind of life you want to live (perhaps a simple life, uncomplicated, comfortable, calm and happy). Then, before making any decision, ask yourself, "Will this action that I am considering get me closer to the kind of life I want to live, or farther from it?" The key, again, is to think of the far-reaching consequences of your decisions, not just instant gratification.

Here's the catch: **the path of LEAST resistance will often take you farther from your destination than the seemingly more difficult one, but an easy trek in the wrong direction is ultimately far more exhausting and devastating than an uphill climb toward euphoria.**

Every decision you make is important. If you smoke now, for example, you might not be able to donate a lung to your own child in the future. And if you have more money than you need while someone else doesn't have enough to buy food, you're not changing the state of the world; you're contributing to it. There are no shortcuts to anyplace worth going to.

Instead of looking to blame others for your dilemmas, look within. Any circumstance (no matter how devastating it may seem), is not only caused by a past event, but is actually a blessing if we gain wisdom from it. History doesn't have to repeat itself if we can learn from our mistakes the first time around.

Treat every living being, including yourself, with kindness, and the world will immediately be a better place.

If you really want to do something,

you will find a way.

If you don't, you will find an excuse.

—E. James Rohn

Utopia

Imagine the world as a restaurant, and we are all its employees; a group of people who share the vision of a perfect dining experience (great food, wonderful service, and a pleasant ambiance).

Each person has a different responsibility, and no task is more important than the other; it takes the combined effort of everyone involved for the dream of utopia to become a reality. While one person is the cook, another is a server, the other washes dishes, and yet another cleans the bathrooms, but they each do what they can in order to help the restaurant be a success.

The most important (and difficult) aspect of ANY job is to focus on the task at hand, and to not worry whether someone else is doing her or his part.

It is not our place to judge or comment on somebody else's job performance. The minute we become more concerned with what someone else is (or is not) doing, is the minute we fail to do our own part.

We cannot control what anyone else is up to; we can only be mindful of what we can each do individually, and do it well.

This approach is very applicable in our daily lives. I have seen people who drive electric cars get angry with SUV owners, and vegetarians being downright hostile toward their meat-eating brothers. Everything is subject to time, place and circumstance. We do not all ripen, awaken or mature at the same rate, and the opposite of what you know is also true.

Be gentle with yourself, kind to others, and love your neighbors unconditionally (not only if they live according to your beliefs).

Everyone is a genius,

but if you judge a fish on its ability to climb a tree,

it will live its entire life believing it is stupid.

—Albert Einstein

Leave No Trace

One of the practices in the kitchen at the Zen Center is to wash, towel-dry, and put used dishes back where they belong (it's part of the "leave no trace" training).

Other residents occasionally left their dishes in the sink, so I did what I thought was the "right thing" to do and put them back. The Temple Keeper saw me doing it one day and gave me "the look" followed by "the speech."

"How are you helping them with their practice if you do that?" she asked. "Leave the dishes for them to see when they return."

It was interesting to understand that even an act of kindness could have a negative impact, and that sometimes we cause more damage by trying to help because we're not looking at the big picture of what "helping" truly means.

This is why *Buddhist Boot Camp* was written without any "should" statements in it. I am not here to tell you what to do, but rather to convey what I've learned in the simplest terms possible, so that you can apply the lessons in your own life if you want to.

The book's intention is to inspire readers to be the best version of themselves there is, which sometimes means NOT putting other people's dishes away, or else you'll get "the look."

Beyond right and wrong there is a field.

I will meet you there!

—Rumi

LOVE AND RELATIONSHIPS

Love Is the Recognition of Beauty

A flower doesn't stop being beautiful just because somebody walks by without noticing it, nor does it cease to be fragrant if its scent is taken for granted. The flower just continues to be its glorious self: elegant, graceful, and magnificent.

Our Mother Nature has provided us with these immeasurably valuable teachers that blossom despite their short lifespan, stars that continue to shine even if we fail to stare at them, and trees that don't take it personally if we never bow down in gratitude for the oxygen they provide.

We also have an incredible and unlimited capacity to love, but the question is: Can we do it like a flower? Without needing to be admired, adored, or even noticed? Can we open our hearts completely to give, forgive, celebrate, and joyfully live our lives without hesitation or need for reciprocity?

It seems like sometimes we go beyond taking things personally and are noticeably deflated when unappreciated. In fact, devastated, we wilt in sorrow and then attempt to guard ourselves by withholding, using all sorts of protections and defenses. We get hurt (even angry) if our boss fails to recognize an astonishing feat, if a lover pulls their hand away, or when a friend forgets our birthday. Can you imagine a flower copping an attitude for not being praised, or the moon dimming its glow because we're too self-absorbed to notice it more often?

Make an effort to shine **no matter what,** to love unconditionally, and to be a kind and gentle soul (even when nobody is watching).

And, if you're so inclined, hug the next tree you see and say, "Thank you!"

Everything has its beauty,

but not everyone can see it.

—Confucius

What a Healthy Relationship Looks Like

Relationships are often misunderstood to be a simple commitment between two people; a dedication to each other with a sense of belonging to one another. That kind of limited perspective breeds expectations, possessiveness and disappointment, and it reeks of ownership, greed, ignorance, and selfish desire.

A healthy relationship is an agreement between two people to support one another in their spiritual practice. It is a vow to encourage each other's dedication, devotion and path, free from attachment or expectations (yet full of caring and compassion). A healthy relationship is based on unconditional love, not on the need to possess. Although you put plenty of "heart" into it, you lose nothing by giving love away.

If each person is equally dedicated to inspire, create, awaken, and enrich the lives of others, then there is no hidden agenda. It is far less important what one receives from the other than what one can give.

Intimacy would suddenly surpass warmth and tenderness to also include patience, vulnerability, honesty, active listening, understanding, connection, and unwavering trust.

There is a healing power inherent in this kind of union, and it is capable of enabling deep transformation for both people. It is an incredible opportunity to actually practice what we learn (from non-violent communication to meditation, listening, mirroring, authenticity, resolve, radical honesty, appreciation, purpose, equality, celebration and mutuality).

Healthy relationships are a collaboration of sorts: two peaceful warriors spiritually supporting one another on their individual journeys to spread positivity and light.

May we all close the gap between what we believe and how we act in the world.

Love does not consist in gazing at each other,

but in looking outward together

in the same direction.

—Antoine de Saint-Exupéry

My Wedding Day

I got married at the Palace of Fine Arts in San Francisco on September 9th, 1999. I was young, in love, and under the impression that if you "seal the deal" when everything is great, then you don't end up in a marriage like my parents' (described by them as "unhappily ever after"), but rather remain youthful, elated, passionate, and optimistic "for as long as you both shall live." Did I mention I was young and in love?

At the time, neither one of us had any role models for what a healthy relationship looked like, but we had more than enough reasons to be skeptical that any marriage could actually last. (I was a paralegal at a family law firm when we met, and the divorce rate in California was about 75 percent back then.)

We decided not to include "'til death do us part" in our vows. Instead, we said we'd remain married "so long as we both want to stay in this." Our love was unconditional, you see, but our staying together was conditioned upon happiness and willingness to continue. We were in love, but we were very logical about it.

So we got married under that beautiful dome in front of three hundred friends and relatives, and I still have wonderful memories from that incredible night of 9/9/99. The number nine, as it turns out, didn't mean "longevity" after all, at least not for us.

Even though we were together for a couple of years before getting married, we had very different expectations and assumptions about what "marriage" actually meant. This difference in opinion ultimately led to a mutual and civil agreement to separate; an agreement that was reached during a couples therapy session just a few months after the big day. We remained best friends for a handful of years after the breakup, but then the universe took us in completely different directions, and we lost touch.

I spent years trying to reproduce the positive aspects of that relationship with others, and then a few more years practicing celibacy while studying psychology and religion at the same time. I wanted to understand what people believe, and why they believe what they do.

When I heard about an old man who introduced the woman he was with as the woman who walks beside him, I finally understood what Antoine D. meant when he wrote, "Love does not consist in gazing at each other, but in looking outward together in the same direction."

It was clear that I had to redefine what the word "relationship" meant to me, and that two people can actually help one another stay on track instead of lose focus.

I call it a REALationship.

What comes, let it come.

What stays, let it stay.

What goes, let it go.

—Papaji

Feelings vs. Emotions

A friend called me crying one day because her boyfriend had left her for another woman. I couldn't understand why she was devastated. "You want to be with a guy who loves you as much as you love him, right? Someone who would never do this to you, correct? And this guy obviously doesn't fit those criteria, so why are you sad?" It made no sense. At least not to me.

It was clear, right there and then, that my view on emotions is very different from other people's. I view emotions as the potholes on an otherwise smooth path toward euphoria, while my friends celebrate (yet complain about) the ups and downs of their emotional roller coasters. I'm not a mean, cold-hearted or unsympathetic individual; I simply trace back the origin of the pain we feel and, if it's self-inflicted—which it almost always is—I say, "If it hurts when you pinch yourself, stop pinching yourself!"

My friends know me very well, by the way, so when they come to me for guidance they actually expect this kind of a reality check. I can understand, however, how or why my comment would seem brutal to an outsider.

I was taught that feelings naturally come and go (like clouds in the sky), whereas emotions are feelings with a story attached to them. Those emotions can last for as long as we keep feeding the story, and this can go on for years. So when people FEEL sad, I understand, but when they EMOTE sad, I get very confused.

Buddhism teaches us that if we get attached to impermanent things (and feelings are a perfect example of things that are impermanent), then our lives will be full of anguish. But if we live each moment without getting attached to it, then we can eliminate the very cause of suffering right there and then, and joyfully live our lives.

As soon as I started studying the Buddha's teaching I thought, "Now THIS makes sense! It's absolutely brilliant!"

Although it makes logical sense, it also takes years of retraining the mind to see things this way (especially in the heat of the moment). We all feel sad sometimes, or hurt, angry, excited, anxious, even blissful, but it never lasts for very long, and that's okay. When one feeling passes, another feeling will replace it.

It's natural to feel disappointed when things don't work out as you had hoped, but the only natural response when that happens is to move on. Difficult as it may sometimes seem, it's still easier than trying to cling to what is no longer there!

All you can do is remind yourself to let go.

Losing an illusion
makes you wiser than finding a truth.
—Ludwig Börne

Sexual Responsibility

Someone posted the following question on *Buddhist Boot Camp*'s Facebook page: "What is the Buddhist stance on homosexuality?"

The answer is simple: Buddhism has a precept regarding sexuality in general; it does not have a different teaching regarding homosexuality than it does on heterosexuality.

The third Buddhist precept, beautifully translated by Thich Nhat Hanh in his book *For a Future to Be Possible,* is about "cultivating responsibility and learning ways to protect the safety and integrity of individuals, couples, families, and society." It is about respecting your own "commitments and the commitments of others," and not engaging "in sexual relations without love and a long-term commitment." The precept invites everyone to "do everything in [their] power to protect children from sexual abuse and to prevent couples and families from being broken by sexual misconduct."

When a sexual act is an expression of love, loyalty, honesty, warmth and respect, then it doesn't break the third precept (whether the couple is of the same gender or not). As long as there is love and a mutual agreement between the two people involved, it isn't sexual misconduct.

Unfortunately, as is the case with all organized religions and philosophies, some sects would argue this point, but I don't think the Buddha would. Bigotry wrapped in a prayer is still bigotry, and we don't play that game!

The same answer applied when someone asked, "Can you tell me what the Buddhist views are on women? I saw something very alarming the other day and want to get my facts correct."

Buddhism equally honors and respects all beings (period). If you witness ANYONE making exceptions to that rule, those exceptions are illegitimate.

The Buddha fully prepared us for this when he said, "Don't believe everything you see, read, or hear from others, whether of authority, religious teachers or texts. Find out for yourself what is truth, what is real. Discover that there are virtuous things and there are non-virtuous things. Once you have discovered for yourself, give up the bad and embrace the good."

So just remember: **Compassion has no contingencies.**

It doesn't matter who you love,
where you love, why you love,
when you love or how you love;
it only matters that you love!
—John Lennon

How a Short Talk Can Make a Big Difference

Carol lived in the same town as her two kids (now in their twenties), but she didn't really like living there. Though she wanted to move closer to her friends in California, she was worried that her children would feel abandoned if she left.

Both kids knew how miserable she was, so they actually wanted her to move, but they were afraid that she would feel rejected if they encouraged her to leave, so they never said anything.

After hearing all sides of the story for months, I finally suggested that we all get together for a mediated constructive talk, which is something they'd never done before.

In just thirty minutes, Carol confessed how guilty she felt for leaving the kids with their father when they were younger. She explained why it had been important for her to walk out of that abusive relationship when she did, and that this was why she was reluctant to leave even now, thinking that having abandoned them once before was enough.

The daughter started to cry, reassuring her mom that she had never blamed her for leaving their father. She had witnessed the abuse firsthand and thought her mom had done the right thing by walking out.

When the son spoke, he confessed that he had always blamed himself for his parents' divorce. He didn't know that it is actually very common for the youngest child in any separated family to feel this way. Hearing his mom's story provided him with a whole new perspective on his own life and personal relationships.

In the end, both kids gave Carol their support in her decision to move to California, and the son is now a spokesperson against spousal abuse and for the importance of respecting women.

We all have fears, anxieties, shame, and regret in our hearts, yet we rarely share these intimate details with the people we love. If we're truly committed to maturing as individuals and as a community, we've got to start being vulnerable with one another. So if you think it's time to have a serious talk with your family, then start by setting some ground rules that keep it a safe place for everyone to share without being interrupted, judged or blamed.

There is no finger-pointing in non-violent communication, and no "should" statements. You might even want to have a mediator present to help keep the conversation calm and focused.

Be gentle with one another, and never nullify what someone holds in their heart. Listen with empathy, and speak with compassion. Healthy communication can open many doors and dispel assumptions we didn't even know we had.

Apologizing doesn't always mean that you're wrong and the other person is right. It just means that you value your relationship more than your ego.

—Anonymous

The Healing Power of Love

If you think that love isn't enough, try going without it for a while and you'll see that it's everything. There is a love-shaped hole in our lives, and no amount of money will ever fill it.

Friendships nurture our hearts with that love, just as trees nourish the earth with oxygen. Good friends, therefore, are like a rainforest of affection.

Just as anyone would drown without air in their lungs, someone in depression is suffocating without love in their heart. You never know when a random act of kindness could literally save a person's life.

So make an effort to meet your neighbors, get to know your co-workers, and befriend your classmates. A stranger is simply a friend you haven't met yet.

Never underestimate the healing power of love. It is just as important for our survival as the food we eat, yet it's free and available in unlimited supply.

Love is the strongest medicine.

Love is the only force capable of
transforming an enemy into a friend.
—Martin Luther King Jr.

RELIGION/SPIRITUALITY

A Simple Definition of God

How do we know for certain that things we cannot see truly exist?

Look at a picture of food, for example. The flavor, texture and scent are not in the photograph, but we know they're there.

Our eyes detect only three dimensions (just as a camera captures only two), so whatever it is that makes life happen must exist in a dimension we simply cannot see. The energy that keeps us alive is beyond our five senses and very mysterious. Even though it is out of our control, we trust that it will wake us up tomorrow morning.

Whether we admit it or not, what we have is faith. We have tremendous faith that this unseen energy will keep the earth spinning, the grass growing, and our hearts beating five minutes from now. We don't know this; we trust it.

Some people refer to this life force as "God," while others call it "the Universe," "Emptiness," "Mother Nature," or "Father Time." The name you give it doesn't matter as much as the appreciation you have for it.

God is not "out there" for us to pursue; God is in our heart to discover.

I believe in God,

only I spell it Nature.

—Frank Lloyd Wright

The Divinity Within

When inviting friends over for dinner, we try to cook something special and make sure the house is clean and tidy. We serve the meal on the dining table with some music in the background, and maybe even light a few candles to create a relaxed atmosphere. We have an innate urge to ensure that someone else's experience of our home is pleasant, comforting and enjoyable. The question is this: Why do we rarely treat ourselves with the same dignity and respect as we do others?

Next time you prepare a meal for yourself, instead of eating it while standing next to the refrigerator (or hovering over the sink), sit down for a few minutes. Turn off the blaring television in the background, clear off the dining table, and embrace your own worthiness of the same ambiance that you offer guests.

Just as when we say, "Namaste," meaning the divinity in us acknowledges and respects the divinity in others, pay homage to the God within you, and celebrate your greatness every day.

You, yourself, as much as anybody
in the entire universe,
deserve your love and affection.
—The Buddha

The Danger of Scripture

Every religious scripture documents someone else's experience of God. Inspiring as the text may be, reading it is not the same as experiencing divinity firsthand.

Let's take romance novels, for a similar example: they do a great job describing love as it was experienced by somebody else, but reading them or watching romantic comedies is quite different than actually falling in love.

Just as everybody's encounter with love is different, so is each person's experience of the divine—that is, their personal relationship with God.

Insight comes to different people at random ages in a multitude of ways. Your altar may have pictures of Jesus, the Buddha, Gandhi, Mother Teresa, the Dalai Lama, Martin Luther King Jr., and Tyler Durden all at the same time, because they are not in disagreement with one another. In fact, as Desmond Tutu and Karen Armstrong constantly remind us, the world's religious leaders are not at war with one another. And as the Charter for Compassion points out, the principle of compassion lies at the heart of all religious, ethical and spiritual traditions, calling us to always treat others as we wish to be treated ourselves.

So do not limit the possibility of your experiences to what you have read in books. If you do, you might dismiss an encounter with God as simply bumping into a stranger on the bus. Divinity is in all beings, including you.

Scripture can be inspiring—but also dangerous, if you confuse it for the real thing. Admire the teaching, not the teacher.

Do not just read about generosity; BE generous. And do not just talk about patience, compassion and unconditional love; make them a part of your daily life!

Your beliefs don't make you a better person;

your behavior does.

—Anonymous

Pray, Meditate, or Both?

Meditation is a method of training the mind to remain calm despite the continuous flux of external conditions. Prayer is a way of expressing our deep appreciation to God, Mother Nature, or the Universe at large for the gift of life.

A true prayer is one of gratitude for the blessings in our lives; it is NOT a time to be greedy or to beg for more. We already have everything we need in order to be happy. So even saying, "God, please give me strength," implies that we don't already have it (when we actually do). Simply say, "Thank you for the strength," and you will be empowered to tap into its unlimited supply.

By being grateful for what we have, we generate energy toward more of the same. So don't focus on what you DON'T have, because energy flows where attention goes (meaning that you would just wind up with more of what you don't want). Meditate to keep your mind firmly fixed in the right direction, and it will raise your awareness of things to be grateful for in your prayers. See the beautiful relationship between the two practices?

A common question is, "What's the harm in praying for world peace?" The problem lies in the idea that it's somebody else's responsibility to make peace happen. Peace begins with YOU. So if you want to know how close we are to world peace, look within.

Prayer and meditation are both wonderful. In fact, reciting a prayer is a common meditation practice. Take the prayer of Saint Francis of Assisi, for example, as I understand it:

Where there is hatred within, train your mind to sow love; where there is injury, pardon; where there is doubt, faith; where there is despair, hope; where there is darkness, light; and where there is sadness, joy. Do not so much seek to be consoled as to console; to be understood as to understand; or to be loved as to love; for it's in giving that we receive, it's in pardoning that we are pardoned, and it's by letting go of the concept of a separate "self" that we are born to eternal life.

If the only prayer you ever say
in your entire life is "thank you,"
it will be enough.
—Johannes Eckhart

Leading by Example

Jesus was virtuous, had tremendous faith in love's capacity to heal, and believed in peace and brotherhood (much like Martin Luther King Jr., Gandhi and John Lennon, all of whom were murdered for trying to dispel our fears by proclaiming the restorative capacity of forgiveness, compassion, patience and unity).

We mistakenly worship the teachers instead of the teachings, idolize them to have been more than mere humans, and construct beautiful but unreasonably exaggerated tales of their lives. This wouldn't be a problem, per se, if the significance of their leading-by-example didn't get washed out in the process.

The best way to express our faith is to live as they did. Love your neighbors (which includes all beings of all walks of life, not just those who speak your language and have the same color skin); be kind to everyone; give; forgive; let go of greed, hatred, and ignorance; be passionate and compassionate; and trust that God knows what She's doing (and that there isn't anything that God isn't or can't be).

The name you give God is not as important as the appreciation you have for it.

May we have gratitude for the teachings, put our trust in the process, and avoid extremes. It is an incredibly beautiful world we live in, with much to be grateful for.

You need not wait until December 31st to make resolutions, nor do you need to be at church in order to pray. Just express your appreciation for life itself by loving God, yourself, and others.

Make THAT your resolution, and you will never know fear.

Every day is the birth of a new you. What are your New You Resolutions?

> There are, strictly speaking,
> no enlightened people;
> there is only enlightened activity.
> —Shunryu Suzuki

Karma

Someone once tried to explain the laws of karma (the laws of cause and effect) by using a metaphor. They asked us to imagine a figure in the sky that not only watches everything we do, but rewards us with blessings for our good deeds, and punishes us with bad luck for each harmful act.

While the intentions of that metaphor were sincere, **karma isn't judgment; it's consequence.** WE are the ones responsible.

If you steal from someone today, for example, it must be because you don't fully understand the pain of being robbed (for if you truly did, you wouldn't steal). You essentially set the universe in motion to cause someone else to steal from you one day, so that you can understand what it feels like.

This will happen again and again (over multiple lifetimes) until you finally understand and vow to never steal again. Come to think of it, this can be seen as a wonderful reward, for you are given the opportunity to learn something new. It is therefore good practice to think of everyone we meet as a teacher.

Buddhism not only honors everyone's path, but respects where everyone currently is on their path. That is why we don't have a list of commandments, so to speak, but a gentle invitation to be more mindful and aware.

If you want to familiarize yourself with the precepts of Buddhism, I recommend reading Thich Nhat Hanh's literary gem, *For a Future to Be Possible*.

What lesson have you learned in the past but haven't yet vowed to never do to someone else (or to yourself) again?

Can you start today?

> How people treat you is their karma;
>
> how you react is yours.
>
> —Wayne Dyer

The Message, Not the Messenger

I remember the first time I ever heard the Dalai Lama speak. He was talking about Self-Control, Determination, and Freedom from Anger, and that was exactly two years after I'd had the same words tattooed on my chest.

Although I never had a name for what I initially thought was my own collection of beliefs and philosophies, it became clear that I wasn't alone. Do I call it Buddhism or Compassion? And is there a difference?

"Kindness is my religion," he said, and I still believe that it's as good a label as any.

I became mesmerized by Thich Nhat Hanh, Jack Kornfield and Dan Millman, but whenever I spoke to my teachers and said something like, "I just love Neale Donald Walsch and Pema Chödrön. Aren't they amazing?!" they would just look at me with a gentle smile and say, "Be careful there."

I knew what they meant: focus on the teachings, not the teacher.

Today, with Facebook being an amazing platform and communication tool, we are all students and teachers, and there are many messengers out there, but the message is always the same; the message is LOVE.

The best way to truly honor our teachers is to do as they did, and spread the love.

Take *Buddhist Boot Camp,* for example. I am not a teacher; I'm a sharer. All I do is tell you what I've been through, and sometimes you get something out of it. The chapters in this book, and the messages I post on Facebook, are journal entries that I have decided to share with the world. When somebody else's story resonates with us, we realize that we're not alone, and we are more alike than we care to admit. This is an important step in breaking down our illusion of separateness, and bringing us closer together.

The Buddha was not a God. He never claimed to be a God, the son of God, or a messenger of God. He was a man who gained clear perspective of the world through nothing more than human effort. And if he was able to do it then, we can do it now!

Being enlightened isn't something you "become"; it is something you continually do! The dictionary defines it as having or showing a rational, modern, and well-informed outlook. It is determined by your behavior, not your beliefs. So go out there and practice being the best version of you there is.

Not all those who wander are lost.

—J.R.R. Tolkien

Buddhism as a Windshield Wiper

Buddhism is often misunderstood. I remember my own dad telling me that he thought we worship "the fat guy" statue that he is accustomed to seeing at Chinese restaurants.

"Buddha" literally means "the awakened one," and there are a lot of Buddhas, not just one. Many sages have awakened from the illusion of separateness, which is what we are all capable of doing, and that's why you too are a Buddha (we're just asleep and trying to wake up, that's all).

The Indians have their own depiction of the Buddha, as do the Thai, the Japanese, and, of course, the Chinese, whose Buddha you often see at restaurants with kids running around him. In each case it is simply a cultural depiction of absolute Happiness the way they understand it, nothing more.

What I really like about Buddhism is that the Buddha was a simple man, not "holier than thou" or something we could never be. He was just like you and me. He wasn't a God (although some sects refer to him as "Lord Buddha"), nor was he special in any way until the figurative lightbulb over his head turned on. Once he understood how the universe was interconnected, almost everyone thought he was crazy (some still do). But a few people realized he was on to something—something beautiful—and so his teachings started to spread to neighboring countries (and continue to).

As is the case with any idea once it is shared, there are many different variations—sects—of Buddhism, and some even contradict one another. Remember playing "broken telephone" in first grade? Same concept!

Buddhist Boot Camp, however, is non-sectarian, sticking to the simple principles as they were prior to being infused with the surrounding culture; some flavor from different teachers has inevitably stuck, but I'm trying my best.

Is Buddhism a religion? That depends on how you define "religion." There is no "God" theory (in the sense of a creator), and any reference to God is to the divinity within all beings (leaving no sentient beings behind). So if it is a religion, then it's like no other.

I think of Buddhism as a philosophy, or a school of thought. You can be Christian or Jewish, for example, and still find the Buddha's teachings helpful and motivational.

In the smallest nutshell I could possibly find, the Buddha taught that we cause our own suffering when we get attached to impermanent things. We cling to people, health and youth, even though we intellectually know that nothing lasts forever. That's why the concept of "letting go" is so fundamental to Buddhism. Acknowledge everything that passes by like a cloud in the sky: some are beautiful, fluffy, and make us smile, while some are dark and cold—but they're all impermanent.

There is beauty to impermanence, but it can only be experienced without attachment, when we enjoy each moment knowing full well that it will pass and make way for a new one. Only then can we actually celebrate every breath instead of feeling sad about what has passed or what will never be again. As Tyler Durden not-so-delicately put it, "Know. Not Fear. Know that one day you are going to die." That distinction, as far as I'm concerned, is the key to happiness. You can choose to be happy, or you can choose to be afraid . . . but the choice is always yours.

There are no commandments to adhere to, so to speak, or rules that failure to follow would dub you as a "bad Buddhist." Not all Buddhists are vegetarian either; the Buddha himself supposedly died from eating a bad piece of pork. There is nobody sending you to hell for what you do, but there are natural consequences to every action (cause and effect . . . karma).

Compassionately understand that everyone is on his or her own path and, furthermore, honor where everyone is on that journey at every moment. No fear, no hatred, bigotry or animosity, just deep understanding, empathy, love, and respect for all beings.

We are all born with the ability to clearly see the world without judgment, and to be amazed by its beauty and wonder. After years of being surrounded by greed, ego, selfishness and fear, however, our vision gets clouded and we can no longer see that we are all the same despite our differences.

So when you think of Buddhism, think of it like a windshield wiper, cleaning up the mess that has dirtied up your eyes; and the more you read—the more you use that windshield wiper—the more moments of clarity you're going to have, and the happier you will be. I promise!

Spiritual practice doesn't make your life longer; it makes it deeper.

I am your brother, whether you realize it or not, and I love you, whether you agree with me or not.

Humility doesn't mean thinking less of yourself; it means thinking of yourself less.

—C. S. Lewis

Teaching Kids How to Think,
Not What to Think

As a kid, Bible study was mandatory where I went to school, but I remember coming home at the age of eight and telling my parents that I didn't believe everything in that book really happened.

Thankfully, that's when my father gave me the key to think for myself. "You don't have to believe everything you read, son," he said. "Just think of the Bible as a book like *Snow White* or *Cinderella,* okay?"

Relieved by this freedom of choice, I said, "Well, in that case, it's a great book with wonderful stories and lessons. I like it!"

I continued reading the first testament until I moved to the United States, where I was introduced to many other religions, which I began to study with equal enthusiasm.

When I discovered the following quote by the Buddha, it reminded me of what my father had told me when I was young:

"Don't believe everything you see, read, or hear from others, whether of authority, religious teachers or texts. . . . Find out for yourself what is truth, what is real, and you will discover that there are virtuous things and non-virtuous things. Once you discover that for yourself, give up the bad and embrace the good."

There is a difference between what we intuitively know is true and what we've been told by others to accept as the truth. I encourage you to never stop contemplating that difference!

I am not what happened to me.

I am what I choose to become.

—Carl Jung

Everyone Is Your Teacher

My parents disowned me when I was eighteen because they didn't approve of who I had involuntarily fallen in love with. I remember trembling from the obscenities flying across the room when they finally yelled, "You're dead to us!" And for three years, I was.

It was actually okay to not have them in my life for a while, but I was not okay with "I hate you" being the last words I would potentially ever say to my father. So I showed up at his workplace unannounced after all those years, and he dropped everything he was doing to hug me and apologize. "I just want you back in my life," he said, and we started from scratch right there and then; not as father and son necessarily, but as friends.

My mother, on the other hand, is a different story. We've had some good moments in the past, but she still clings to grudges and resentments from her childhood, so you can imagine how fresh something as "recent" as seventeen years ago must be.

Interestingly enough, I'm very grateful for both of them. While my father continues to show me what letting go looks like, my mother's behavior has taught me equally valuable lessons on how NOT to be. It's sad, really, and I hope she starts forgiving people she believes have wronged her in the past, and that one day she decides to forgive me too. Resentment is poisonous to our health, and it pains me that she suffers so much.

Please don't be so quick to shut the door on people with whom you've gotten into arguments in the past. Disagreements aren't conflicts unless pride and ego get involved, and people DO eventually grow out of those. Sometimes they just need to know that you have already forgiven them, and that it's okay for them to approach you.

It's true that we get comfort from those who agree with us, but we are offered opportunities for tremendous growth and maturity from those who disagree with us. This has taught me to value everyone as my teacher.

Life becomes easier
when you learn to accept an
apology you never got.
—Robert Brault

A Pseudo-Problem with the Golden Rule

The sentiment behind the golden rule is great (treating others the way we wish to be treated ourselves). But nowadays we don't even treat ourselves very well! We knowingly consume things that are bad for us, continue working at jobs we hate, and don't spend half as much time relaxing as we do stressing.

Come to think of it, we ARE treating others the way we treat ourselves: poorly! We feed our children junk food, opt for cheap instead of quality even when it matters, rarely give anyone our undivided attention, and demand a lot more from others than what is reasonable or even possible.

Let's try something new: let's treat everybody as if we just found out they're about to die. Why? Because it seems that's the ONLY time we slow down enough to get a new perspective on life—either then or when we have a near-death experience ourselves. Be gentle, patient, kind and understanding.

We're all headed in the same direction, so let's start treating each other better along the way!

I want you to be concerned about your neighbor.

Do you know your neighbor?

—Mother Teresa

UNDERSTANDING

The Opposite of What You Know Is Also True

You don't have to agree with, only learn to peacefully live with, other people's freedom of choice. This includes (but is not limited to) political views, religious beliefs, dietary restrictions, matters of the heart, career paths, and mental afflictions.

Our opinions and beliefs tend to change depending on time, place, and circumstance. And since we all experience life differently, there are multiple theories on what's best, what's moral, what's right, and what's wrong.

It is important to remember that other people's perspective on reality is as valid as your own. This is why the first principle of *Buddhist Boot Camp* is that the opposite of what you know is also true.

No matter how certain we are of our version of the truth, we must humbly accept the possibility that someone who believes the exact opposite could also be right (according to their time, place, and circumstance). This is the key to forgiveness, patience, and understanding.

That said, tolerance does NOT mean accepting what is harmful. Oftentimes the lesson we are to learn is when to say "no," the right time to walk away, and when to remove ourselves from the very cause of anguish. After all, we are the ones who create the environment we live in.

While staying with different host families around the world over the years, I noticed that people's definitions of everyday words like "comfortable" and "clean" were often very different than my own. The opposite of what I considered true proved to be just as true for others, which was very humbling.

If two people can have very different definitions of what "walking distance" means, imagine bigger words like "right," "wrong," "God," and "love."

What the caterpillar calls the end of the world,

the master calls a butterfly.

—Richard Bach

Rewriting the Stories We Tell Ourselves

I visited my teachers' sanctuary on the Big Island of Hawaii for a weeklong retreat a few years ago, humbled to be in the presence of greatness with the opportunity to ask about the meaning of life, spiritual practice, and monastic ordination.

When my friend and I arrived at their organic farm and settled into the yurt they had arranged for us to sleep in, I was immediately torn by two very opposing reactions to the place: On one hand, I thought it was the most beautiful and peaceful home I had ever seen (it was secluded, quiet, and surrounded by koi and lotus ponds, Buddha statues, Tibetan prayer flags, and exotic fruit trees on the border of the property, next to a stunning bamboo forest with a view of the ocean and the neighboring island of Maui). But on the other hand, I wasn't one for camping. Unreasonable as it may sound, I had a terrible fear of bugs, and I was extremely uncomfortable sharing a living space with them.

It's silly, I know, but I was raised in concrete homes that were regularly sprayed to draw a definitive line between the wilderness outside and the bug-free environment for humans on the inside. At the farm, however, that line was blurred and sometimes non-existent. So instead of feeling calm and serene at the sanctuary, I curled up in the fetal position and constantly felt like something was crawling on me.

My friend suggested that I talk about my anxiety with our hosts, but I thought she was crazy. "Here I am," I said, "with the opportunity to tap into their deep wisdom, gained from years of studying with gurus all over the world and silent retreats in the caves of India, and you want me to ask them about my fear of BUGS?!"

I shook my head and said, "No way, it's too embarrassing."

Just then our hosts walked into the yurt carrying a pot of split-pea soup, steamed vegetables and quinoa, and joined us for supper by the altar.

Listening to their spiritual guidance, I felt like we might as well be sitting around a campfire in biblical times, hearing the word of God from the mouths of sages . . . it was majestic.

"Don't you have something to ask them?" my friend suddenly said out loud, and I wanted to magically disappear to avoid the ensuing conversation. But there was nowhere to go and my invisibility cloak wasn't working. ☺

"How do you guys do it?" I asked. "There was a scorpion-sized spider in the bathroom; there are crickets and centipedes everywhere; frogs, bees, and who knows what else is crawling on the other side of this glorified tent! While I'm extremely grateful that you guys invited us here, I don't think I can stay. I have to leave!"

With very few but carefully selected words of wisdom, they skillfully invited me to rewrite the story in my head about bugs. They adjusted my perception to better understand that perhaps the insects weren't invading "my" space, but maybe

I was invading theirs. "Who was here first?" they asked me, and I immediately realized that they were right. The spider was 1/100th my size and probably more terrified of me than anything else. They suggested that if I tried naming the bugs as I saw them (Richard the centipede or Maya the bee), I would shift my consciousness to accept each animal as someONE, not someTHING.

After a week on the farm with more opportunities to practice this new perspective than I care to admit, I realized that my fear was simply a learned behavior from watching my mother react to insects when I was growing up.

As soon as I found that "page" in my mind where I wrote that bugs are bad, I was able to erase it and write in something else instead: "All sentient beings are equal."

I still don't find bugs adorable or have a pet tarantula or anything. But a year or so later, while visiting my parents in their sterile home environment, I noticed that a small spider had managed to get into the house, and crawl onto my hand while I was having a conversation with my dad. Without even realizing what I was doing, I let the spider crawl onto my other hand and said, "Hey there, little guy . . . are you lost?"

I calmly took him outside where he leaped off my hand and onto the grass. I suspect he probably spent the next thirty minutes cleaning himself because an "icky human" had touched him.

When I sat back down to continue the conversation with my dad, he stared back at me in complete shock.

Isn't it refreshing to know that just because we've always been a certain way, it doesn't mean we have to stay that way forever?

Our beliefs are merely stories in our minds that we ourselves wrote long ago. Knowing that, don't you feel empowered to rewrite them if they no longer serve you?

Scan your mind for viruses called fears, anxieties, judgments, doubts, hatred and despair, and put a little note next to them that says "Outdated; no longer valid."

> I've learned so much from my mistakes,
>
> I think I'm gonna go out there and
>
> make some more!
>
> —Anonymous

One Man's Truth Is Another Man's Blasphemy

I used to think of God, the Bible, religion, Jesus, and the church as one thing. So when I started questioning the validity of the church or the Bible, I started doubting the existence of God—and that's just silly; they have nothing to do with one another.

It is very possible (and perfectly okay) to believe in God but not the Bible, to be religious but never go to church, and to even downright hate the church and religion, yet love God. Why? Because they have nothing to do with one another! One of the greatest misconceptions is that we have to believe in all of it or in nothing at all, which is why many people choose nothing at all (it's certainly easier and more appealing than getting caught up in the confusing dogma).

This is challenging to explain, so please bear with me, and refrain from picking at what words simply make impossible to convey, but I'm gonna try anyway.

As I understand it now, "God" is not a creator nor responsible for the existence of things (we don't know what is), but it's the unseen energy that keeps our hearts beating and our lungs functioning. It is completely out of our control, yet we trust that it will wake us up every morning. Whether we admit it or not, we have tremendous faith that this energy will keep the earth spinning five minutes from now. We don't know this; we trust it. We have faith in "God," but that faith has nothing to do with religion, the Bible, or, least of all, the church. And the name you give this God doesn't matter as much as the appreciation you have for it.

Buddhism is different from other religions in that there is no "Creator/God figure," nor a theory on how the world came into existence. If you ask any Buddhist how the world began, he would simply say, "I don't know." You just gotta love that kind of honesty!

The Bible is a story depicting somebody else's experience of God (the unseen energy described above). More precisely, the Bible is the story of someone else's explanation of what they understood somebody else believed many years prior, before that story was translated, transliterated, edited, copied, and morphed for over 2,000 years of multiple revisions.

Religion is what happens when someone takes the concept of God as described in scripture (as a creator), and orchestrates a story about why we're here and for what purpose.

As for the church? Well, it's a business. And like any business, its business is to stay in business. It is easy to dismiss the church altogether because you'd think there would be some consistency in what they teach and there isn't.

Many churches do amazing, incredible, and wonderful things to help people of all walks of life, but some churches still preach hatred and judgment, so it has naturally become easier to do away with the church altogether than to try and make sense of it. I truly feel bad for the churches that do good in the world. because the other ones taint their validity. This is why I encourage everyone to do good without any affiliation, but simply for the sake of doing good.

As for Jesus . . . I love the brother! I have said this before and I will say it again: he was virtuous, had tremendous faith in love's capacity to heal, and believed in peace, brotherhood, and understanding. Whether he truly existed or not doesn't matter. We mistakenly worship the teachers instead of the teachings, and even idolize them to have been more than mere humans. We construct beautiful but unreasonably exaggerated tales of their lives, which wouldn't be a problem, per se, except that the significance of their leading-by-example gets washed out in the process.

As Gerry Spence says, "My intent is to tell the truth as I know it, realizing that what is true for me may be blasphemy for others."

We need not agree with, only learn to peacefully live with, other people's freedom of choice. This includes (but is not limited to) political views, religious beliefs, dietary restrictions, matters of the heart, career paths, and mental afflictions.

That said, tolerance does NOT mean accepting what is harmful. So may all beings live in peace, and may all beings be happy.

You can safely assume

that you've created God in your own image

if it turns out that your God

hates the same people you do.

—Anne Lamott

Repentance

In my life . . .

I have been selfish, resentful, and unapologetic;

I have cheated on almost every person I've been in a
relationship with;

I have not always respected the commitments of others;

I have killed two cats;

I have physically beaten and badly hurt a dog;

I have gone fishing with my father;

I have lied to my parents, friends, lovers, teachers, employers,
the government, and strangers;

I have cheated on school exams;

I have copied somebody else's homework;

I have broken many traffic laws;

I have stolen;

I have gossiped;

I used to be homophobic;

I used to burn ants and spiders with a magnifying glass as a
child, and killed other insects throughout my life by other
means;

I have said some harsh words that I can never take back;

I have discriminated against people based on looks;

I have wished ill upon others;

I have used guilt to manipulate;

I have been greedy;

I have been ignorant;

I have condoned acts of war;

I have condoned the act of killing animals with my dietary choices;

and I have consumed drinks and foods that are toxic to my health.

There is no excuse for any of it.

I am sorry.

If you do not openly repent your wrongdoings, you are more likely to repeat them.

—Cheng Yen

Still Learning

Patience is the most challenging practice for me as an adult.

When I was growing up, the surest way to upset my dad was to stand idly with my hands in my pockets. "It's a sign of laziness," he would say. "Do something!"

I now realize that I was essentially taught from a very young age to do everything fast, and to do it correctly, or I would upset the "higher-ups" and suffer the consequences. Perhaps it's natural, then, that I was drawn to working at law firms as a young adult; they are fast-paced, cold, brutal, unforgiving, demanding, and . . . well, a lot like boot camp!

After a decade as a paralegal and legal secretary, however, I too grew cold. Not only did I really like the directness of being told exactly what to do without any sugarcoating, I started treating others with the same level of rigidity. It was efficient, after all, and the golden rule says to "treat others the way we wish to be treated ourselves," right?

Wrong.

The golden rule doesn't apply if we ourselves want to be treated like a machine. I never understood why people couldn't "take it like a man," so to speak. And I can still hear my parents yelling, "I'll give you something to cry about!" and it makes me quiver.

Sadly, I ruined almost every relationship in my life because of this unbending mentality, and it was only after living in a monastery with wonderful teachers who made all the right observations that I finally understood what was going on.

I went from being abused to being abusive, not only toward others, but also toward myself.

The upside to this is that CHANGE IS ALWAYS POSSIBLE.

Awareness was the first step (clearly understanding why I was the way I was, and then vowing to change it), but habitual tendencies are tough to break, and changing them requires something I'd never been taught before: patience.

Life is an ongoing classroom in which everyone is our teacher, and every situation contains a lesson for us to learn. It is only by first being patient with myself that I can ever learn to be patient with others.

I don't blame my parents for raising me the way they did (it's all they knew because they were probably raised the exact same way), and I certainly don't blame the legal industry for operating the way it does (I'm the one who chose to be in it, after all, until I chose to get out).

Some law firms, I hear, are actually moving away from that working style and implementing non-violent communication techniques in the workplace. And let's face it, if there is hope for lawyers, then there is hope for us all! (My apologies to attorneys everywhere, who always end up being the butt of a joke.)

We make our own choices, and we pay our own prices. That's why a few years ago I decided to be gentle, kind, patient, understanding, loving and compassionate, and I'm right there with the rest of you guys: still learning.

Thank you for your patience.

A lesson will repeat itself until you learn it.

—Anonymous

Middle Ground

When things don't go as we had hoped, we either look for external influences to blame instead of reflecting on what we could have done differently, or we go too far in that latter extreme and blame ourselves too much.

There is a happy middle ground wherein we consider possible outcomes if we had done things differently, but we don't call ourselves failures or losers just because we didn't have all the facts right off the bat.

It's very easy to spot these extremes when other people go off on a tangent, venting about everything that went wrong without seeing what they could have done differently, but the trick is to catch ourselves when WE do it.

We bend over backward to reason with ourselves so that we can feel better about what happened, but even if we walk away from the experience feeling justified, we don't walk away from it any wiser.

When others beat themselves up about doing everything wrong, we immediately steer them in the other direction by reminding them about other factors that were in play. So why can't we do it with ourselves when WE feel like complete losers?

I guess that's why having honest friends around is so important. They tell it to us like it is (whether we want to hear it or not), and if we're wise enough, we take all the comments into consideration, learn, grow, mature, and try again.

If you want your life to be a magnificent story,

then begin by realizing that you are the author,

and every day you have the opportunity

to write a new page.

—Mark Houlahan

The Beauty of Gray

I made the decision to live a simple and uncomplicated life a few years ago, and I thought it meant having to diligently eliminate anything that interfered with that goal. As a result, I swung like a pendulum for a few years, flying from one extreme to another, not realizing that serenity isn't found at either end of the spectrum, but actually somewhere in between.

When you're not standing at either end, but hanging out in the middle instead, nothing can offend you. Compassion and deep understanding toward others are significantly easier to access when nobody is far away from where you are.

So go ahead, surround yourself with like-minded people for comfort and support, but don't forget to honor those who push your buttons just as much if not more, for they're the ones who provide an opportunity to grow and mature beyond having buttons that can be pushed.

The world isn't black-and-white, I now know. We live mostly in the gray.

Kīnā'ole: one Hawaiian word says it all.

Doing the right thing, in the right way,

at the right time, in the right place,

to the right person, for the right reason,

with the right feeling . . . the first time!

Live and Let Live

I stayed with different people in different cities on my journey across the country, and one thing proved to be universally true: we all create much of our own suffering.

There was one host, for example, with whom you'd think I would have royally gotten along because we were both into yoga, were big fans of farmers' markets, were vegetarian, environmentally conscious, etc., but there was a big difference between us that wasn't evident on paper: he was an activist who literally fought and protested against anyone who didn't hold the same values as he did, and I am not. He was angry with people who ate meat, for example, with drivers who had gas-guzzling cars, and even with me for not being angry with them too! It was very interesting.

I completely understand why people eat meat—for example, it tastes good! But my choice to stop eating it back in the nineties didn't turn my meat-eating brothers into enemies (nor do I try to convert other people to my way of life by telling them that what they're doing is "wrong").

If people who know me are compelled to change their diet or athletic lifestyle to resemble my own in the hopes of getting similar results, that's great, but it's not my job to judge anyone who doesn't.

It is my way of leading by example. Some follow; some do not. *C'est la vie.*

When I was staying in Florida for a short while, my nieces woke up one morning and asked me to make them breakfast. "What would you like?" I asked, and they said, "Scrambled eggs, Uncle T!"

This was a true test. I could say, "No way! I don't eat eggs, and you shouldn't either!" or I could simply ask, "Would you like some toast with that?"

I prepared their eggs just as they requested, and when they asked, "How come you're not having any?" I explained to them what being vegan means, and why I was eating something else. They smiled, nodded, and then said, "That's cool!" as they went on eating their breakfast.

The seed of option was planted. They were introduced to a different lifestyle because they inquired about it, not by force. In time, with the right conditions, those seeds will sprout and grow, and my nieces will make their own decisions. A week later, in fact, they tried a fresh fruit smoothie for breakfast and really liked it!

My life is my message, you see. Even the *Buddhist Boot Camp* Facebook page and book, for example, are not things I'm PUSHING on anyone else; I am simply sharing my life with all of you who CHOOSE to be a part of it, which is what I love about this medium the most. What you do with the message is your choice.

We do not always agree on everything (nor do we have to), but we do understand the importance of being kind to one another, not judging each other, and seeing one another as human beings trying our best.

Who was it who said, "Live and let live"? I think they were onto something!

If you recall the happiest moments in your life, they are all from when you were doing something for somebody else.

—Desmond Tutu

Voting

Voting is not something that we do only once every four years; it's a daily way of life. We vote with our wallets through every purchase decision that we make (be it at the grocery store, department store, or online businesses). For example: there is only one reason why grocery stores in Hawaii sell mangoes that are imported from Ecuador: people keep buying them. Tropical fruit grows right here on the island, but we can't blame the stores for supplying what we demand. If we change our ways and only buy local mangoes, however, then they will only sell local mangoes; it's that simple.

If you're against animal cruelty, for example, yet purchase toothpaste made by a company that tests its products on animals, you're essentially supporting a cause that you don't believe in. Remember: your beliefs don't make you a better person, your behavior does! We vote when we pay for services too, not just products. If you're against violence but rush to the movie theater to watch the latest violent blockbuster, then more movies that glorify the act of war will be produced, thereby adding more violence to the world.

Take inventory of your decisions' far-reaching consequences, and make sure they are in line with your values. Bridge the gap between what you believe and how you act in the world.

You're not stuck in traffic; you ARE traffic.

We blame society, but we ARE society.

—Anonymous

SUCCESS

True Luxury

Have you noticed how we view every situation from a relativity perspective? We immediately contemplate ways to make things different than they are, be it better, faster, bigger, warmer, bolder; it's exhausting! Now imagine letting go of labels and evaluations, and allowing everything to be just as it is, without wishing for it to be any other way. Accept yourself, and then others, without needing to change anything.

Feelings and emotions will inevitably continue to rise (both pleasant and unpleasant). *Buddhist Boot Camp* is simply reminding you to relax, to acknowledge that everything is temporary, including youth, health, and life itself. All experiences are as transient as clouds in the sky: anger comes and goes, excitement rises and falls, and tears dry on their own. So practice tenderly watching your feelings and emotions as they move in and out of your mind, just like traffic on a busy street.

Remain aware of what goes on around you, but try to do it without the mind's commentary. Observe without judgment, and experience life without resistance.

Opinions change, perspectives widen, and the opposite of what you know is also true. Take a step back and you'll see that all of our anguish is self-inflicted. We assign meaning to everything, and simply refuse to accept it all as impermanent.

Instead of spending so much time thinking about what's missing from your life, remind yourself (if only for twenty minutes a day), of everything you already have: from a comfortable bed to sleep on, to a roof over your head, to clean air, drinking water, food, clothes, friends, functioning lungs, and a beating heart.

When you approach each moment with gratitude, not only will you stop experiencing life from a place of lack, you will experience abundance!

THAT is luxury. THAT is being rich!

Some people are so poor,
all they have is money.
—Anonymous

Careers Are Overrated

I was working in Corporate America, sending creditors a thousand dollars of my salary every month to slowly pay off my outrageous credit card debt, and one day I realized that I was only a couple of payments away from being debt-free for the first time in my adult life.

"What am I going to do with that extra thousand dollars a month after my debt is paid off?" I wondered. My mind started racing with all sorts of crazy spending ideas, but then I had one of my big AH-HA Moments and decided that I didn't actually have to make that "extra" thousand a month. I could quit my job, change my lifestyle, work less, and live more!

It became a fun game of "How little can I live off of and still have a great time?" Moving to Hawaii was an obvious choice at the time (even though many people consider it to be a really expensive place to live), because everything I enjoy doing outdoors, like tennis, volleyball, hiking, biking and kayaking, is not only fun and free, but I can do it all year round!

I sold everything I ever owned, moved to Hawaii with no savings account, but no debt either, filled with determination to live a simple and uncomplicated life.

That was over six years ago, and I'm still having a great time.

True, I could have continued working a full-time job and used the "extra" money to help others, but there are many ways to help people that don't involve money (like volunteering my time, skill, talent and devotion). An old lady alone at the hospital after a stroke, for example, doesn't necessarily need money; she needs a hand to hold, and I can do that now that I only work part-time!

A nine-to-five job is not the only way to spell success.

Man sacrifices his health in order to make money.

Then he sacrifices money to recuperate his health.

And then he is so anxious about the future,

that he does not enjoy the present moment.

As a result, he does not live in

the present or the future;

he lives as if he is never going to die,

and then he dies having never truly lived.

—The Dalai Lama,

when asked what surprises him the most

When to Walk Away

I worked for a software development company in the early nineties with managing partners who used to scream and cuss at us, literally throw piles of paper across the room and yell, "File this!" and constantly fight with each other in front of everybody. I hated my job so much that I used to cry in the bathroom on my breaks. I stayed there for a year because I thought having that company's name on my résumé would be impressive, but as it turned out, the company folded a month after I left and nobody ever cared that I worked there.

Buddhism teaches us to be tolerant and accepting, but tolerance does NOT mean accepting what is harmful. Even if you think there are benefits to staying in a situation that is harmful, I urge you to reconsider. Abuse is never justified, and it is only when we don't love ourselves enough that we allow others to treat us with disrespect. When you love yourself, you can do anything with dignity and be appreciated for it, or you can take your skills elsewhere.

Success means being happy, and nobody deserves to hate what they do for a living. So love yourself enough to choose happiness every time, and you will be the most successful person in the world!

Tolerance does not mean accepting what is harmful.

—Timber Hawkeye

Success Means Being Happy

If working a full-time job leaves you feeling like you're only living part-time, is it possible that careers are overrated?

Nobody looks back on their life and says, "I should have spent more time at the office," so why do we make work our priority? If it's because we regard those who work really hard and earn a lot of money as successful, then let's reevaluate! They tend to have a lot of stress in their lives, high blood pressure, heart problems, ulcers, headaches and insomnia . . . Does that sound like success to you?

The only folks who truly love their jobs are the ones who have found their calling. Have you found yours? A nine-to-five job is not the only way to spell success, you know. Don't let the concept of change scare you as much as the prospect of remaining unhappy!

The thesaurus lists a "calling" as another word for career, and it's nobody's calling to hate what they do for a living. If success means being happy, are you on the right track?

The difference between who you are

and who you want to be

is what you do.

—Anonymous

Redefining "Enough"

Sure, it would be nice to eat out every night, sleep on a much more comfortable mattress, have a fancier phone and computer, a massage chair, and the ability to travel more frequently, but I don't want to work 40 hours a week to be able to afford all that.

I don't feel that I sacrificed those things by choosing to work 20 hours a week; I simply exchanged them for what I personally want even more: getting off work at noon, going swimming, hiking, volunteering, playing tennis and volleyball, writing, reading, you name it. I wouldn't be able to do all that with a 40-hour-a-week job, and "things" don't make me happy, but all that free time sure feels great for my health (mental, spiritual, physical and emotional).

It's a question of what you want MORE out of life, and whether your daily decisions reflect your answer, ya know?

We make our own choices; we pay our own prices. Some people love their full-time jobs, and I think that's awesome. But what if more people switched to a 20-hour workweek? We would immediately double the number of people employed, and they would automatically be twice as happy with all that free time to spend with their family and friends. Am I crazy for thinking that we need THAT a lot more than we need to buy more STUFF?

There is a difference between the cost of things and the price of things. The COST of a new smart phone, for example, is about $400, but the PRICE is about two weeks of work (if your salary is similar to mine).

I get a lot of e-mail from people who say things like, "I really hate my job and want to simplify my life, but I NEED this job to pay for my car insurance, car payment, cell phone bill, mortgage, living expenses, etc." My answer simply reflects back that the smart phone, car payments and other extras are all choices that we make, and the price we pay for those things isn't in dollar value so much as what we have to DO in order to pay for them.

Go a whole day without complaining—then a lifetime!

One day you will wake up
and there won't be any more time
to do the things you've always wanted to do.

Do them now!

—Paulo Coelho

A Simple Life

My dad told me this story when I was a little kid, and even though many of us have heard it before (it was originally told by Heinrich Böll), I believe it deserves to be regularly shared, especially at every high school graduation around the world. Enjoy!

One summer, many years ago, a banker was vacationing in a small village on the coast. He saw a fisherman in a small boat by the pier with a handful of fish that he had just caught. The businessman asked him how long it took him to catch the fish, and the man said he was out on the water for only a couple of hours.

"So why didn't you stay out there longer to catch more fish?" asked the businessman.

The fisherman said he catches just enough to feed his family every day, and then comes back.

"But it's only 2 p.m.!" said the banker, "What do you do with the rest of your time?"

The fisherman smiled and said, "Well, I sleep late every day, then fish a little, go home, play with my children, take a nap in the afternoon, then stroll into the village each evening with my wife, relax, play the guitar with our friends, laugh and sing late into the night. I have a full and wonderful life."

The banker scoffed at the young man, "Well, I'm a businessman from New York! Let me tell you what you should do instead of wasting your life like this! You should catch more fish to sell to others, and then buy a bigger boat with the money you make so you can catch even more fish!"

"And then what?" asked the fisherman. The banker's eyes got all big as he enthusiastically explained, "You can then buy a whole fleet of fishing boats, run a business, and make a ton of money!"

"And then what?" asked the fisherman again, and the banker threw his hands in the air and said, "You'd be worth a million! You can then leave this small town, move to the city, and manage your enterprise from there!"

"How long would all this take?" asked the fisherman. "Fifteen to twenty years!" replied the banker.

"And then what?"

The banker laughed and said, "That's the best part. You can then sell your business, move to a small village, sleep late, fish a little, play with your kids, take naps in the afternoon, go for an evening stroll with your wife after dinner, relax, sing, and play the guitar with your friends. You would have a full and wonderful life!"

The fisherman smiled at the banker, quietly gathered his catch, and walked away.

Live simply so that others may simply live.

—Gandhi

Knowing Is Not Even Half the Battle

You never make the same mistake twice. The second time you make it, it's no longer a mistake; it's a choice. What we essentially are is a series of bad decisions.

If knowing alone made us wise, then every senior citizen would be a Zen master. Attaining realization is not about what we know, but what we do with that knowledge. Meditating for sentient beings to be freed of their suffering doesn't make you a Buddhist any more than simply thinking about buying a lottery ticket makes you a millionaire. So treat every person in need as an invitation to be of service, and then you'll be putting compassion into action.

Buddhist Boot Camp urges you to roll up your sleeves and actually help anyone in need; and to align your habits with what you already know is best. It all begins with you and the decisions you make. Start with behavior patterns, food choices, and deciding how to most effectively use your time, money and talent to benefit others.

Pretend every person you meet is the Buddha, and you won't be greedy, hateful or disrespectful toward anyone. Stop trying so hard to always be right or to prove yourself superior to others, and strive to connect with people instead. We are all in this boat together. Answer me this: What is detrimental to your health? Why are you still doing it?

All know the Way, but few actually walk it.

—Bodhidharma

ANGER, INSECURITIES,
AND FEARS

At the Root of Our Suffering

To reduce the amount of stress in our lives (as well as anger, fear, disappointment, anxiety and intolerance), we must start by reducing our expectations.

If you get road rage because of slow-moving traffic, annoyed with bank tellers for taking "too long" with other customers, hurt feelings when a friend forgets your birthday, or disappointed when the weather doesn't clear on the day of your planned picnic, take note that most of your expectations are completely unreasonable and self-centered.

When we don't expect a movie to be incredible, we're not totally disappointed if it falls short of amusing. Not hitting the jackpot in Las Vegas isn't a big deal if we don't expect to anyway; and, for adults, it's actually okay for a book to have an unhappy ending. Without expectations, we're not completely deflated if our blind date turns out to be rude, or when an avocado is brown on the inside. Think about it: the only reason you're not disappointed when you don't find a love letter in your mailbox every day is because you're not expecting to find one in the first place.

With the people closest to you, a simple agreement to never intentionally harm one another is sufficient to solidify a healthy and long-lasting friendship. And when we expect so little from one another, we are actually inspired to do more.

Be patient with the employees at the grocery store and the servers at restaurants. They might be moving slower than you expect because they're sick or have a headache, and it's possible that they just received some bad news, or that it's their first week on the job. The problem isn't how fast or slow they move; the problem is your expectation. They might even be working with a disability of some sort that prevents them from moving faster. Be patient.

We're jaded by a society that promotes overnight delivery, express checkout lines, 24-hour customer service, airplanes, carpool lanes, instant rebates, instant messaging and instant coffee. Constantly encouraged to expect what we want, how we want it, and right away, we are conditioned to move more quickly, multitask, speed-read and drive through, which leaves no room in our lives for learning patience, tolerance, listening, or conscious breathing.

Slow down, people, smell the plumerias, and chew your food!

Then, and only then, will you be in a position to be kind to yourself and others.

When you release your expectations
that the world should fulfill you,
your disappointments vanish.
—Dan Millman

The Origin of Anger

Anger is like a mask that covers hurt feelings or fear. So next time you are angry, see if you can trace the origin of that feeling to its root of disappointment, shame, fear, hurt, impatience or embarrassment. Learn to skillfully explain THOSE emotions instead of the anger, and you'll quickly find peace from understanding the misunderstanding.

It has somehow become socially acceptable to publicly express frustration and irritation by yelling, slamming doors, giving someone the finger, or storming out of the room. For some reason, however, sensitivity and vulnerability are still frowned-upon as signs of weakness (especially with men), even though honesty and grace are significantly more courageous than a bad temper.

If we use anger to motivate change and fuel determination, it can actually drive our good intentions forward without causing any harm. But when anger isn't handled with care, it can turn into hatred and rage, and that's not only unproductive, it's dangerous.

When you're disappointed or irritated, take a moment to think about what you would like to accomplish, and you'll find that screaming or acting out will rarely, if ever, get you the results you're after. EXPLAIN your anger, don't express it, and you will immediately open the door to solutions and understanding.

Many people say this is "easier said than done," but when you contemplate the ease or difficulty of any practice, don't forget to consider the challenges of the alternative. As difficult as it may be to express our insecurities in a healthy way, it is far more damaging to lose our temper or keep everything bottled up inside. Remember the Freudian advice, "Pain does not decompose when you bury it."

Gratitude is the antidote to anger. We cannot be angry and grateful at the same time (one stomps the other). So choose gratitude every time, as it never fails to put the mind at ease.

> No one can make you feel inferior
>
> without your consent.
>
> —Eleanor Roosevelt

The Two Wolves

It's as if there are two versions of me: one is calm, truthful, giving, forgiving, harmonious and wise, and the other is sometimes greedy, selfish, dishonest and argumentative. So when I wake up every day, I say good morning to both of them, but then I vow to only listen to the wiser of the two for the rest of the day.

What's funny is that the selfish part of me is loud and obnoxious, always yelling, "Listen to me, listen to me!" while the selfless side just quietly sits there like a Buddha, with a knowing smile on his face, thinking, "You know what to do . . ."

I believe that both of these parts are within each of us, and that we are capable of being either one. The choice is ours with every decision we make.

It's like the Native American story of the old man who told his grandson, "There is a battle between two wolves inside all of us. One is Evil (it is anger, envy, greed, resentment, inferiority, lies and ego), and the other is Good (it is joy, peace, love, humility, kindness, empathy and truth)." When the boy asked, "Which wolf wins?" the old man quietly replied, "The one you feed."

It is better to have a mind opened by wonder
than a mind closed by belief.

—Gerry Spence

Note the Antidote

I approach fear the same way I approach almost everything else in life: with an antidote. Here's what I mean: anger and gratitude, for example, cannot coexist in the same thought; it is cognitively impossible. The moment you are angry with your spouse, for example, is the moment you stop being grateful for having them in your life in the first place; yet the moment you go back to gratitude, the anger goes away. It's like magic: gratitude is the antidote to anger.

Here's the trick: instead of focusing all of your energy on "letting go of anger," focus on increasing your gratitude . . . and the anger will naturally subside.

Fear also has an antidote, and I hope you can follow my train of thought here.

I spent years envious of people who had faith because I was too logical to understand it, which was frustrating because I'd heard it said that if you feed your faith, then all your fears will starve to death, and now I know it's powerfully true.

"Faith" is trusting the process. You see, SOMETHING is making your heart beat right now, your lungs function, the grass grow and the planets spin. So whether we admit it or not, what we have is FAITH. We have faith that our heart will keep beating, and that we'll wake up tomorrow morning. We don't KNOW this; we TRUST it. So trust the process and honor it by not overlooking this tremendous faith that you have. It's okay. It doesn't mean your faith has to be wrapped up in religion. I, Timber Hawkeye, for example, am Faithfully Religionless.

Why is acknowledging our faith so important? Because faith is the antidote to fear.

We now know that energy flows where attention goes. So if you feed your fears they get bigger, but if you feed your faith, your fears have nothing to eat and eventually die. The problem is that fear has been drilled into us from a very young age, with its level of severity greatly varying depending on our upbringing, culture, family, etc.

So in your "battle against fear," I say change direction: don't focus on letting go of fear; focus on increasing your faith . . . and the fear will disappear on its own.

It's like kundalini yoga, if you've ever done it. It involves a lot of very rapid breathing and can get very frustrating if you're trying to breathe in and out really fast. As my yoga instructor says, however, just focus on the exhale; the inhale will happen automatically.

Trust the process, my friends. Let it happen (it's going to happen anyway). When you trust the process, you trust that it's okay for people to be different from one another, that as much as we don't like it, there's a reason for what's happening in the world, and the opposite of what we know is also true. Trust. The. Process.

There is balance and harmony in the world (the north and the south poles), and we need it so that we don't spin out of control, right?

So just focus on feeding your faith and the fears will naturally go away. Try the breathing stuff . . . I'm serious. Close your mouth and breathe in and out through the nose really fast. It can get tricky UNLESS you just focus on the exhale and trust that the inhale will happen effortlessly.

Being nice to those you don't particularly like

is not being two-faced;

it's called growing up.

—Anonymous

It's Never Too Late

Angela always dreamed of seeing the world outside of her hometown. She imagined living in a small apartment somewhere, waking up to the feel of the sun on her face.

Instead of making the decision to move, however, she spent her life riding out every situation, which meant staying with her husband until he decided to leave, working the same job for fifteen years, and only buying a new car when the old one died. She didn't realize that NOT making any decisions is a pretty big decision in itself.

Her sister Bonnie, on the other hand, pursued a career as far away from home as possible, and her best friend Joy went on a trip across Europe, where she decided to stay.

Something as small as making a decision can be very empowering. We feel in control of our situation (rather than victimized by it), and when things change, we change with them. This flexibility and fluidity doesn't happen overnight. There is a gap between needing to make a decision and actually making it, and that gap is almost always filled with fear. We fear change and the unknown, so we cling to a past that's already gone and attempt to avoid a future that is inevitable.

Knowing that this is our problem, however, doesn't solve it. This is where we can draw inspiration from people everywhere who live by a different set of rules. They don't live in a different world than the rest of us; they just look at the same world from a different perspective.

Bonnie was filled with confidence and courage, for example, and Joy didn't pack fear into her suitcase for the trip to Europe (she left it at home). Angela intellectually knew that if her sister and best friend could do it, she too could make some serious changes in her life, and she finally did!

First things first: she turned off everything in her life that filled her with fear, doubt, paranoia, anxiety and anguish (i.e., television). It was a big change for her, since she habitually watched the morning news before going to work and also listened to talk radio in her car.

True to form, the news provided her with more than enough anxiety for the day, every day, without fail (be it an outbreak of a new strain of the flu, a gunman at the mall, food poisoning from spinach, a security alert at the airport, a storm on the horizon, high-fructose corn syrup in her coffee, or a medical report linking hair dye to breast cancer).

If that wasn't enough, Angela was also used to watching the ten o'clock news before going to bed at night, which, strangely enough, actually made her feel grateful to still be alive, since everyone else seemed to have either been murdered, raped, robbed, or gone missing while she was at work.

After donating her television to a nearby home for the elderly, she canceled her newspaper subscription and began reading books about the art of happiness instead. She called Bonnie and Joy on a regular basis, and they were thrilled to hear about the changes she was making in her life. They encouraged her to continue cultivating whatever filled her with love, light, and positivity, and eliminating everything that filled her with fear (including her friend Gretchen, who was suspicious of everyone trying to either steal her identity, take advantage of her, or tap into her computer).

Angela gathered enough courage to quit her job, move out of New Hampshire, and go back to school. She discovered the mood-elevating benefits of nutrient-rich foods, and now teaches yoga on the beach in Honolulu.

Today she is a daily inspiration for many tourists who take her yoga class at the resort. Angela encourages them to break their routines, make decisions, and change their lives.

Bonnie and Joy recently surprised Angela by showing up on the beach during one of her yoga classes to celebrate her birthday.

Never discourage anyone
who continually makes progress,
no matter how slow.
—Aristotle

Controlling Your Temper

Practice listening to other people talk about their beliefs without interrupting them. Listen to Catholics, Jews, Buddhists, Mormons, Anarchists, Republicans, KKK members, Heterosexuals, Homosexuals, Meat Eaters, Vegans, Scientists, Scientologists, and so on . . .

Develop the ability to listen to ANYTHING without losing your temper.

The first principle here at *Buddhist Boot Camp* is that the opposite of what you know is also true. Accept that other people's perspectives on reality are as valid as your own (even if they go against everything you believe in), and honor the fact that someone else's truth is as real to them as yours is to you.

Then (and this is where it gets even more difficult), bow to them and say, "Namaste," which means the divinity within you not only acknowledges the divinity within others, but honors it as well.

Compassion is the only thing that can break down political, dogmatic, ideological, and religious boundaries.

May we all harmoniously live in peace.

You will not be punished for your anger;

you will be punished by your anger.

—The Buddha

Insecurities

While hanging out by a friend's swimming pool, my mother passively said to me, "Looks like someone is getting chunky!"

I was sixteen and far from obese by any measure, but I must have already been insecure about the few extra pounds I had gained, because I started seriously obsessing about my weight after that.

Within a month I had her take me to a sporting goods store to buy an Ab Roller (the most popular body-sculpting contraption back in 1993). When she asked me, "Why do you want this?" I said, "Because I want to be a stripper one day!"

She laughed, of course, assuming I was joking, but I felt like the only way I could officially overcome the "chunky issue" was if people paid me to take my clothes off.

It turned out that my insecurity had nothing to do with my outward appearance after all, because even when I started stripping in a couple of years, with a killer six-pack and a fake tan, the pale fat kid still stared back at me when I looked in the mirror.

I'm not blaming my mother for doing anything we don't all do every single day. She may have said it to me only once, but I continued calling myself fat and unattractive for years thereafter every time I looked in the mirror.

Your words have tremendous power—even the words you say to yourself—so please choose them wisely.

Your past mistakes guide you, not define you.

—Anonymous

The Pain Behind Our Fears

As her health and memory started to fade, my friend's grandmother moved out of her home and into her daughter's house for closer observation.

We all thought it would be a wonderful idea for me to take care of the property (now that nobody was living in it), and perhaps even rent out a room or two, and have the money go toward Grandma's expensive medicine and care.

The house had fruit trees in the back yard, as did many houses in that neighborhood, and my plan was to collect the excess from the community and feed those in town who couldn't feed themselves. With the abundance of food that would otherwise go to waste, nobody was to go hungry again.

My friend and his wife had known me for many years and blindly trusted me to always work for the benefit of others. Strangely enough, however, when we approached his parents, aunts, and uncles with the proposal that I accept this unpaid caretaker position in good faith, and that I do everything I could to ease the family's burden of worrying about the property, help with its upkeep and cleanup, and, of course, make sure everybody had a wonderful home to visit when they were in town, everyone thought it was a great idea except for my friend's mom, who couldn't see past her fears and lack of trust in other people (let alone a stranger).

She was worried that I would intentionally burn down the house or something, and sue the family for all they had, or that I'd illegally sublet the rooms and pocket the rent, trash the place, or—and this she said with a great deal of sinister humor in her voice—if I really was as kind and generous as her son made me out to be, I would (God forbid) let homeless people sleep on the floor when it was cold outside.

As it turns out, there was a lot of pain behind her fear. There always is. Any talk of someone living in her mother's house just made the fact that her mother was dying a reality for her to have to accept, and she clearly wasn't ready to do that.

I flew back and forth to meet with everyone, and I even had an attorney draft an agreement that gave me no rights to any money or lawsuit under any provision whatsoever, with the intention to best protect the family's interest and, most importantly, Grandma's integrity, but her daughter still wouldn't budge.

This was very frustrating and sad to me at the time, and I did not understand why she wouldn't accept someone's generosity without thinking there was a "catch."

Has the majority of our population gotten this cynical, jaded and pessimistic and I haven't noticed? Do people no longer believe in random acts of kindness and giving? If that's the case, then we need to do more of it so that people believe again!

Please don't be discouraged by this story, but let it ignite the fire in your heart to give, forgive, and believe.

A perfectly wonderful house is now a graveyard for cockroaches and geckos, falling apart because of mildew and neglect, which is what I imagine has happened to my friend's mom's heart as well.

The important lesson I learned from this experience is that you can't want something more for someone than they want for themselves, and that some people simply don't believe in the light. (How could I have been so naive as to not know this before?) It doesn't matter if you shine light in their faces, because if they don't believe in it, they won't see it.

I realize now that it's way more important to open our hearts than our eyes. If our hearts are closed, then it doesn't matter what we're looking at—we would never see everything as it truly is: Buddhaful.

People don't need a reason to help people.

—Anonymous

LIVING IN GRATITUDE

Grateful for Each Breath

The phrase "Take a deep breath" is misleading. The breath isn't something we can just "take."

Breathing is a gift, a miracle, offered to us over and over again, yet much like our health, we often take it for granted right up until the moment we no longer have it. Let's accept this gift with gratitude and appreciation as we would all presents, by saying, "Thank you."

Sometimes society can seem disgruntled and ungrateful, and the world may appear to no longer be appreciative, but some of its people still are, and therein lies the promise.

So go ahead . . . accept a few deep breaths with your eyes closed and a smile on your face.

What a joy it is to be alive!

> Being content makes poor men rich;
> discontentment makes rich men poor.
> —Benjamin Franklin

Prevention Is the Best Cure

I reached the end of my rope one day and finally said, "Enough is enough! I've had it with your lies, violence and manipulation, so get out! This relationship is OVER!"

So even though we had grown up together and shared some good laughs over the years, it felt REALLY good to finally walk away from that abusive relationship. The newfound freedom gave me an opportunity to grow as an individual, do some soul-searching, read books, and spend a lot more time outdoors.

The first few weeks apart were pretty difficult, I have to admit. I really missed the routine of coming home to that familiar embrace (because we humans are comforted by routine, even if it's dysfunctional). But now that it's been more than ten years since we last saw one another, I can honestly say that I don't miss my TV at all. ☺

It's true that not EVERYTHING on television is negative, bad, violent or filled with mind-numbing commercials, but I personally had to cut it out altogether in order to end the addiction. Did I miss out on some amazing footage, lessons and research shared on the Discovery Channel, for example? Absolutely! But I certainly didn't miss waking up to bad news or going to bed with even worse news, that's for sure! I did my own research instead, at my own pace, on my own schedule, with no commercial interruption.

The only change I initially noticed was that I couldn't join the conversation with co-workers standing around the water cooler at the office anymore, but after a decade without TV I noticed a significantly more remarkable change: all of my thoughts were my own. I wasn't being told what to think, what to buy, like, eat or watch; I was making my own decisions.

I wonder if not being exposed to media is part of why I'm so happy all the time. I mean, I didn't just cut out TV; I went all out and eliminated newspapers, radio, and magazines too!

In a book called *Meditation,* Eknath Easwaran explains how we don't just eat with our mouths; we eat with our eyes and ears too. So if we watch or listen to poisonous negativity, violence, gossip, and pretty much anything that is not conducive to our growth or maturity as adults, then it's no different than eating only refined sugars, fried foods and saturated fats; we're bound to get sick. That sickness, however, takes the form of fear, paranoia, anxiety, greed, insecurity, a lack of trust in our fellow brothers and sisters, and discontentment with life altogether. Yuck!

Luckily for us, as is the case with most ailments, prevention is the best cure!

Start paying attention to how much of what you watch is filling you with fear, anger or anxiety, versus how much of what you read or expose yourself to is about unconditional love, gratitude, trust, respect, and the divinity within all beings (including yourself).

As Carlos Castaneda said, "We can make ourselves miserable, or we can make ourselves happy. The amount of work is the same."

So go ahead and choose to be happy by taking the first step of avoiding the very things that make you UNhappy. It certainly helped me!

Flowers only bloom when they are ready.

People are the same way.

You cannot rush or force them open

just because you think it's time.

Be patient.

—Timber Hawkeye

Versions of Violence

When I first confronted my mother about being abusive, her response was, "Where? Show me a bruise!" It's strange how she never hit us to the point of leaving a visible mark, but the scars ran deep, and the abuse wasn't always physical. I was thirteen at the time, mind you, and couldn't articulate how scared I was of my own parents.

It wasn't until I saw a poster at the supermarket that advertised a local help-line for abused children that I even knew it was illegal for parents to beat their kids.

A couple of decades later, I heard the song "Versions of Violence" by Alanis Morissette, and it made me realize how I too was being violent as an adult without even knowing it.

The song gave me an opportunity to self-reflect and grow, which I'm deeply grateful for. Unsolicited advice, coercing, controlling, labeling, judging, and meddling are just a few versions of violence that deeply affect us. "These versions of violence," Morissette writes, "sometimes subtle, sometimes clear. And the ones that go unnoticed, still leave their mark once disappeared."

Everything in your life will improve
as soon as your determination to move forward
is stronger than your reluctance to let go of the past.
—Timber Hawkeye

You're in Charge!

When I was growing up I used to cry in my room and try to think of ways to either kill myself or the people I blamed for my misery to make it stop.

I ended up doing what I later discovered is the Buddhist approach to alleviating suffering: I didn't get rid of my mother, for example; I got rid of my emotional attachment to her. There is a cause for our suffering, and there is a way out.

It turns out that I hated her because she never met my expectations of how I thought a mother "should" be. But as soon as I took away those expectations, I finally saw her as my greatest teacher, not enemy, and accepted the fact that she did the best she could.

Although she didn't model behavior that I wanted to mimic when I grew up, she perfectly demonstrated what I DIDN'T want to ever become, and that's an equally important lesson.

What I learned is that nobody is in charge of your happiness (or unhappiness) except YOU!

When somebody loves you,

they don't have to say it.

You can tell by the way they treat you.

—Anonymous

Why Gratitude Is So Important

Once upon a time, on a cold winter morning, I rolled out of bed after not being able to sleep all night. The neighbors had been arguing and slamming doors, thunder and lightning kept waking me up, and I couldn't get comfortable in any position. I got up cranky and frustrated, and my day was just beginning.

The real kicker? Two months earlier a friend had suggested that I try meditating every morning! To tell you the truth, I absolutely hated it. I mean, for years I'd kept the same routine of coffee, news, breakfast, and going online to check my e-mail. Now, before doing anything else, I had to sit for a few minutes and focus on my breath? Most times I just ended up thinking about all the other things I'd rather be doing (or simply wishing I was still in bed).

As you can imagine, sitting down to meditate was extremely difficult after a sleepless night, but a promise is a promise.

I got out of bed, went to the little corner in my apartment that I had set up for meditation, and sat with my bitter thoughts about everything that had kept me up at night.

Within two minutes of sitting down, however, something interesting happened: none of my complaints would stick. Instead of being upset about the storm outside, I felt blessed to be indoors. The neighbors' arguing only made me feel grateful for the healthy relationship I was in, and when I really thought about it, there was no way I could complain about being uncomfortable in my bed while so many people were sleeping in cardboard boxes on the street every night!

It was amazing how gratitude managed to stomp every negative feeling I had. My morning meditation turned out to be better than a cup of coffee, and I was positively enthusiastic about the day ahead. In fact, when I ran into my neighbors on the way out, I felt sorry and sad instead of angry, because I knew they'd actually had a rougher night than I had.

Gratitude is an amazing antidote to almost any negative feeling. The minute we are angry with someone is the minute we have momentarily forgotten how grateful we are for having them in our lives in the first place. And as soon as we return to gratitude, the anger disappears. It's amazing!

Try it out sometime and you'll find that smiling is inevitable.

> If you find yourself in a hole,
> the first thing to do is stop digging!
> —Will Rogers

A Simple Way to Be the Change

We used to rely on the church to instill a sense of gratitude in our children, but as many people have strayed away from religion for one reason or another, it is now up to you and me to use whatever tools we've got to talk about everything we're grateful for on a regular basis.

By spreading gratitude on Facebook and Twitter, for example, we balance out the fears and anxieties that the media instills in society through every other channel and station.

Let's show the next generation how easy it is to find things to be grateful for. The alternative is a terrible and growing sense of entitlement, which is nothing short of an epidemic, if you ask me.

Gratitude is at the core of every chapter's intention to awaken, enlighten, enrich and inspire. I invite you to include gratitude at the foundation of your online posts, daily interactions with your friends and family, and even lunch conversations at work. Keep a gratitude journal or create a gratitude wall in your home where everyone can write things they're grateful for on a regular basis.

Next time someone complains about their job, for example, be the one to say, "I'm grateful that I have a job." And if someone whines about not having enough of something, be the one to say how much you appreciate what little you've got. I'm not suggesting that you be obnoxious to the point of invalidating other people's version of the truth, but you can simply and skillfully steer them in the direction of the silver lining because trust me, they want to see it too, they just can't at that moment. Be patient without condoning their negativity. Skillful means.

You get the point: don't support this growing problem of people taking things for granted and feeling like victims; instead, celebrate the fact that we are far beyond survival and actually spoiled compared to so many others!

Seeking happiness outside ourselves
is like waiting for sunlight
in a cave facing north.
—Tibetan saying

Thoughts, Words, and Actions

If you've ever taken a puppy for a walk, you know that it runs after everything that sparks its curiosity. After we train it to obey some simple commands, however, it grows to be our obedient and intuitive best friend.

The mind can be just as active and difficult to control as a puppy, yet we've never trained it to listen to us. Why haven't we done this? Our mind chases random thoughts, jumps to conclusions, and has a hard time staying focused. We have so little control of it, in fact, that sometimes we can't even turn it off at the end of the day. If it were a puppy, we would be very upset!

We know that Buddhism is about training the mind, and that there are many methods of doing so. The second principle of *Buddhist Boot Camp* is that our thoughts become words, and our words become actions. To train the mind, however, *Buddhist Boot Camp* suggests working backward. Start by changing your actions, then be mindful of your speech, and your thoughts will eventually follow.

First, recognize and eliminate your bad habits (whatever they may be). If you habitually act out of anger, for example, then there's no fertile soil in your mind for the seed of gratitude to grow. To think positively, your actions must be in line with your intentions.

Be part of the solution by not being part of the pollution, for it isn't enough to simply study Buddhism; we must practice what we learn!

Training the mind requires a lot of self-control, determination, and freedom from anger (whether you follow this particular method, transcendental meditation, yoga, or any other approach).

Buddhist Boot Camp is not here to necessarily teach you anything new, but to encourage you to put into practice what you already know; to point you in the direction of gratitude and unconditional love. We can't just THINK ABOUT compassion and kindness; we must BE compassionate and kind. Now let's get to work!

An ounce of practice
is worth more than a ton of preaching.
—Gandhi

Doing the "Right Thing"

Clyde is a single father of two. When his wife died of type 2 diabetes last year, he vowed to take better care of the family's health by doing three new things on a regular basis: eating more fruits and vegetables, exercising, and never getting fast food again.

Tonight, with only ten dollars to spend on dinner, he will make them mashed potatoes, grilled chicken, and steamed broccoli florets. Even though he wants to buy everything organic, he simply can't afford to right now, so he's doing the best he can, avoiding processed foods, soda, and everything else that has high-fructose corn syrup in it.

A woman named Laura is standing behind Clyde at the grocery store. Her life is completely different than his, so her shopping cart is filled with organic and seasonal produce that she can easily afford without hesitation. Although she's a strict vegetarian and a big supporter of local farmers, she can't really be upset with Clyde for eating meat or buying non-organic food. Organic is better than conventional, that's true; but conventional is certainly better than fast food. According to his time, place, and circumstance, Clyde is actually doing the right thing. They both are.

Never judge anyone for the choices that they make, and always remember that the opposite of what you know is also true. Every other person's perspective on reality is as valid as your own, so no matter how certain you are that what you're doing is the "right thing," you must humbly accept the possibility that even someone doing the exact opposite might be doing the "right thing" as well.

Everything is subject to time, place, and circumstance. There are no "shoulds" in compassionate thinking!

Do all the good you can,

by all the means you can,

in all the ways you can,

in all the places you can,

at all the times you can,

to all the people you can,

as long as you can.

—John Wesley

Activism

I met a wonderful woman yesterday who initially came across as a bitter, aggressive, jaded, angry political activist, and outraged feminist. The more I spoke of how I believe world peace begins by looking within ourselves (changing our mindsets to eventually evolve out of greed, hatred, ignorance and fear), the more upset she seemed to get that I wasn't proposing we do anything to change "the corrupt system."

We spoke for a couple of hours before her defenses were dropped long enough to at least understand (but not necessarily agree) that although my approach and hers are completely different, they are to the same end.

"The system," after all, is made up of individuals. By raising the next generation to be peaceful and compassionate, we are building future systems to operate with altruistic intentions instead of hunger for power.

This woman wanted global change to happen NOW, and I admire her for that sense of urgency and passion. We must use different tactics to reach a wide variety of audiences, so although she's a revolutionary activist raising conscious awareness in a very different method than my own, she is, in fact, a soldier of peace in the army of love.

What I learned is that we are all activists in our own way. I may not be protesting with picket signs in an attempt to overthrow governments, for example, but I did write a book, and I am planting seeds of gratitude with the hope of remembering and reminding everyone what "for the people" truly means. I would have never considered myself to be an "activist" before, but I guess I am, in my own way.

Soldiers of peace in the army of love are sometimes difficult to identify as allies, because some use completely different methods than we do. An outsider might have thought that this woman and I were arguing, but I think we were growing, and for that I am forever grateful.

If you invite me to an anti-war rally, I won't go.

Invite me to a pro-peace rally,

and I'll be there!

—Mother Teresa

Permanence

In my twenties I got a tattoo at the end of each one of my relationships. I think it's because I was disappointed and looking for something permanent when everything else felt so uncertain.

Luckily I chose phrases or artistic depictions of things I'd want to believe in forever. They are reminders of what is truly important:

Unconditional Love, Honesty, Respect, Trust, Self-Control, Determination, Freedom from Anger, Happiness, Tranquility, Equality, Strength, Divinity, Freedom, The Spirit of Aloha, Sticking Together, A Sense of Home—and when I realized that all of those were very serious, I added a tattoo of a volleyball player as a depiction of Fun.

Are we all looking for something permanent in an impermanent world?

The moment we accept, not fear, that everything is temporary, we can appreciate each breath as a gift. Whether it's the love of a friend, our family, youth, or life itself, let's celebrate and enjoy that we have it today.

Live as if you were to die tomorrow.

Learn as if you were to live forever.

—Gandhi

The Charter for Compassion

Somebody saw me with my book in hand this afternoon and asked, "Are you a Buddhist?" and I didn't know how to answer that. I am a lot of things, yet not one of them defines me. Although I am technically Jewish, my mantra is Hindu, was ordained Buddhist, and my morning meditation is the Catholic prayer of Saint Francis of Assisi. I study religion and psychology simultaneously (so as to understand why and how people believe what they do), and find myself wholeheartedly agreeing most with the non-sectarian Charter for Compassion, which reads as follows:

The principle of compassion lies at the heart of all religious, ethical and spiritual traditions, calling us always to treat all others as we wish to be treated ourselves. Compassion impels us to work tirelessly to alleviate the suffering of our fellow creatures, to dethrone ourselves from the center of our world and put another there, and to honor the inviolable sanctity of every single human being, treating everybody, without exception, with absolute justice, equity and respect.

It is also necessary (in both public and private life) to refrain consistently and empathically from inflicting pain. To act or speak violently out of spite, chauvinism, or self-interest, to impoverish, exploit or deny basic rights to anybody, and to incite hatred by denigrating others—even our enemies—is a denial of our common humanity. We acknowledge that we have failed to live compassionately and that some have even increased the sum of human misery in the name of religion.

We therefore call upon all men and women to restore compassion to the center of morality and religion; to return to the ancient principle that any interpretation of scripture that breeds violence, hatred or disdain is illegitimate; to ensure that youth are given accurate and respectful information about other traditions, religions and cultures; to encourage a positive appreciation of cultural and religious diversity; to cultivate an informed empathy with the suffering of all human beings (even those regarded as enemies).

We urgently need to make compassion a clear, luminous and dynamic force in our polarized world. Rooted in a principled determination to transcend selfishness, compassion can break down political, dogmatic, ideological and religious boundaries. Born of our deep interdependence, compassion is essential to human relationships and to a fulfilled humanity. It is the path to enlightenment, and indispensable to the creation of a just economy and a peaceful global community.

The one and only test of a valid religious idea, doctrinal statement, spiritual experience, or devotional practice is that it must lead directly to practical compassion.

—Karen Armstrong

Easier Said Than Done

The most common recurring response to the messages in this book is, "That's easier said than done."

This is boot camp, people . . . NOT the path of least resistance.

Training our mind to be more positive, loving, accepting and kind may be "easier said than done," but it's certainly easier than living the rest of your life with greed, hatred and anger!

We have to do the work if we want to free ourselves from the binds of ignorance.

Let go of what's killing you, even if it's killing you to let go!

An easy trek in the wrong direction
is significantly more difficult than
an uphill climb toward euphoria.
—Timber Hawkeye

IN GOOD WE TRUST.

—Buddhist Boot Camp

Sit Happens at buddhistbootcamp.com

If you enjoyed this book, please share a copy with a friend!

When one person spreads the Dharma,
millions of people are taught.

Join our online community
on Facebook (facebook.com/buddhistbootcamp),
and on Twitter (@BuddhistBCamp).

Namaste.